Skinny Budget Marketing

Grow your Business without Breaking the Bank

Skinny Budget Marketing

by Lynn Kinnaman

Published by Works by Design, LLC

*To my cherished
friends and clients -
thank you
for the opportunity to get to know you.*

*May this book
help your
businesses grow and thrive.*

*Special thanks to Amanda for your
support and encouragement,
and Karleen,
for your sharp eye and
invaluable feedback.*

Contents

What is
Skinny Budget Marketing?

Skinny Budget Marketing is making the most of what you have, using effective tools and coordinating your marketing efforts to maximize results without breaking your budget.

This book will show you how. It's a mini-marketing course for the non-technical entrepreneur on using new and traditional methods, digital channels and tested techniques to build your business and expand your opportunities.

I've divided it into five sections: *Preparing, Positioning, Presenting, Promoting and Perfecting.*

These 5P's will take you through the steps to becoming a smart Skinny Budget Marketer.

Small to mid-sized business owners tell me they struggle to prioritize their marketing efforts in their spare time, because running their business is all-consuming.

Their day is full dealing with customers, employees, bills, scheduling, deadlines, taxes, government regulations, etc. Things like social media aren't on the radar.

Their resources are at the breaking point.

The relentless hysteria surrounding the "next best thing" only intensifies the stress.

You have to be on this one, you must do that or you'll be out of business! Here's something new - don't get left behind! If you don't sign up today you will never succeed.

Trying to figure out what to do, how to do it and when to find the time is giving them nightmares.

If this sounds familiar, then I wrote this book for you.

I am not a "guru" - far from it. And I don't have all the answers - no one does, especially is the fast-moving world of Internet marketing. What I do have is a well-developed curiosity and the desire to learn about technology.

Whether you make widgets, run a restaurant or sell flowers, you have to focus first on your customers and your products and services. Since my business is marketing, website building and consulting, my priority is to find ways to help businesses succeed.

I can do what you don't have time for - research, read, attend seminars, webinars and workshops. I experiment, test ideas and make mistakes. In doing so, I learn what works and how much time and energy it takes.

Then I organize and summarize my suggestions and present them in a manageable way, so you can decide what works for you.

There are choices, but it seems all you hear about in marketing today is exclusively social media.

Why is the hype so intense?

There's a saying - *"When all you have is a hammer, everything looks like a nail."*

That means when your marketing toolbox contains only social media, then you apply it to every situation, without considering whether it's the best tool for the job.

If you can imagine trying to remove a screw with a hammer, you can appreciate how limiting that is. You may have the shiniest, biggest hammer, but if you need a screwdriver, you're going to have trouble.

Social media and Internet marketing are not the end game. They are simply among the tools in a business owner's toolbox. To get the results you want, you want the right tool for the task.

Jay Baer of Convince and Convert says: *"The goal is not to be good at social media. The goal is to be good at business because of social media."*

Social media and digital marketing can improve business but only when you understand why you are using them and what you are trying to accomplish.

Before you set up a Twitter account or Facebook page, you want to have a clear idea of what you expect to get from it.

That means knowing exactly what you do, why you do it, who needs it and what makes you uniquely qualified to provide it.

This book will help you do that. The time you spend in preparation is going to pay dividends when you plan and execute your marketing.

UNIQUE QUALIFICATIONS

Each of us has talent, experience and skills that create individual synergy.

There are reasons your customers would rather work with you than the dozen or so others out there that seem to offer the same product or service. Those reasons are your *unique qualifications.*

In a bit, I'm going to ask you to define these for yourself, but first, I'll tell you about mine.

My background includes marketing, advertising and sales and I have been a writer and teacher my entire life. I've run several small business. I've failed, and succeeded, and learned from both.

My unique qualifications are that I have a broad background in marketing, I understand small business, I appreciate non-technical professionals and can translate jargon and communicate in clear terms.

My experiences qualify me in a unique way, and are the reason people choose to work with me.

WHAT YOU'LL GET FROM THIS BOOK

Skinny Budget Marketing will help you understand the concepts and benefits of using social media, Internet marketing and traditional media.

You'll learn how to develop a strategic marketing plan and determine what tactics are best for your objectives.

You'll learn the vocabulary of social media and Internet marketing so you can avoid being bamboozled by social media snake oil salesmen. You'll be able to speak the language, ask insightful questions and make good decisions.

You'll develop a concise business statement, suitable for branding, slogan, tag line and elevator pitch development, and get to know your customer.

You'll understand the importance of content, how to write it and where to get ideas.

You'll have a plan that's manageable and a direction that makes sense.

At times you may find some of the discussion elementary. After teaching numerous classes and working with many clients, I've found it's better to explain than assume. If you already know some of this - kudos to you!

Whether you decide to handle everything yourself, delegate to your employees, or contract outside help, after you finish reading Skinny Budget Marketing you'll understand the trends, terminology and opportunities available.

You won't be left out of the conversation anymore. You'll be an informed participant and enlightened business owner.

Because technology changes so fast, I cover the basics here and have a Resources Section and Glossary for you on my website:

WorksbyDesign.com

This way I can keep it current and update it as needed so you have the latest information. There's a Recommended Reading list and the Skinny Budget Marketing Club newsletter, also.

Owning a business is an experiment. There are no guarantees, no fail-safe formula.

Marketing is the same way. There's no magic system or secret sauce that works every time for everybody. You learn, you apply the knowledge you have, you evaluate it, you make corrections, you increase the things that bring in results and you repeat.

Then you share, grow and succeed.

BEWARE THE JABBERWOCKY

In Alice's Adventures in Wonderland and Through the Looking-Glass by Lewis Carroll, Alice says: *'It seems very pretty,' she said when she had finished it, 'but it's rather hard to understand!' (You see she didn't like to confess, even to herself, that she couldn't make it out at all.) 'Somehow it seems to fill my head with ideas—only I don't exactly know what they are!"*

Information overload can fill you with uncertainty, and there are people out there who would love to use that confusion to pick your pocket.

Once you plant a flag on the landscape of social media, you'll get inundated by self-described experts who promise to get your company on the first page of Google, triple your number of Facebook fans or claim they reviewed your site and identified problem areas they could fix for you immediately.

Just yesterday I got a call from "Facebook", trying to sell me advertising space. I asked her to e-mail the information and so far, not a word.

Be skeptical. And tread slowly when you're told you MUST do this or that, and do it *right now*. Ask them: How do they know? Has the research been done on your business, or with your target customer?

There are some fantastic resources out there and outstanding companies who can help you, and I've listed many of them on my website.

But not everyone is what they seem.

Sonia Simone on Copyblogger says, *"Some of them are selling garbage. Some of them are selling solidly useful stuff. It's all packaged about the same way, which makes it hard to tell the difference."*

The questionable ones give themselves away with pressure tactics, threats and wild promises.

Follow your instincts. Use the same evaluative process you would on any big decision.

Most of all, don't feel pressured to pay someone to do something that you don't understand or they can't explain. If they can't explain it and you can't verify the legitimacy, view that as a warning flag and act accordingly.

Preparing

Once there was only a handful of options in advertising and promotion and they were pricey, but worth it, because consumers were a captive audience.

Everyone read the newspaper. When you needed a phone number, you looked in the yellow pages. Television had three major networks. Radio shows were limited to those in range.

Advertising on these outlets almost guaranteed you'd reach your potential customers.

This kind of media can still be effective but economics and consumer habits have lessened the impact of these methods. Here's what we used in the past.

Your Business Location

At one time, your physical location could make or break you. The saying about the three most important things in real estate were the same for a company: Location, location, location.

In order for customers to do business with you, they had to be able to walk into your building. An obscure address, inconvenient parking or poor signage could kill a fledgling business. However, not everyone could get a good site, or be able to afford a top-notch spot.

Physical location, while important, is less so when people can buy online.

Advertising

Traditional advertising outlets were newspapers, magazines, radio and television. Phone directory listings were considered mandatory for any legitimate business, and outdoor advertising also played a role.

With so many media choices now, it's hard to know which one will reach your market.

Direct Mail

Some might consider it junk mail, but businesses have relied on direct mail marketing to attract and hold customers and it's still a popular option today.

Companies can buy lists of consumers based on demographics or develop their own lists from customers and prospects.

Mailings include circulars, letters, postcards or even free items.

Statistics show that a good response rate on direct mail is between 1-2%. With postal rates increasing, direct mail has become an expensive way to reach people.

Closing post offices and longer delivery time also makes this option less attractive.

Press Releases and Articles

When businesses had a news-worthy announcement they would prepare a press release, named as such because it was sent to the press: primarily newspapers and magazines.

The press had the option of tossing it or using it, so how interesting and relevant it was could tip the scales.

Distribution was limited and time-consuming, but as long as newspapers and magazines were hungry for news, your press release would get noticed, and possibly picked up for a feature article.

In print media, the amount of page space given to press releases, editorials and articles is in direct proportion to the number of ads sold. When ad sales are down, page count is down. There is more competition for precious space.

With fewer ads, there are fewer articles, seriously limiting opportunities.

Odds and Ends

Billboards and signage in venues such as movie theaters or sporting events provide visual reminders of a business, as long as consumers can absorb the information as they zoom past in their car or participate in the activity that brought them to the location.

Imprinted products have always been popular, and work well in some situations, not so well in others. You might have five pens with the names of insurance companies, but is that how you selected the company with whom you do business?

On the other hand, printed clothing, such as tee-shirts and hats, could get your business name in front of hundreds, or even visible on TV, under the right circumstances.

The Ultimate Marketing Tool: Word-of-Mouth

The best promotion a business can have, in the past or today, is good word of mouth.

While you can encourage this by providing excellent service and outstanding products, there has always been a limit to how much influence a business can wield. People who like your product or service may never bother to tell anyone else about it. But if you can get them to, the results can be extraordinary.

Years ago there was a Breck shampoo ad that illustrated this: *"I'll tell 2 friends, they'll tell 2 friends, and so on and so on."* It was accompanied by the model's face being reproduced to illustrate the point.

Social media has taken the concept of word of mouth and changed the dynamic. Bad news spreads fast, too.

Or, as Amazon's Jeff Bezos says, *"If you make customers unhappy in the physical world, they might each tell 6 friends. If you make customers unhappy on the Internet, they can each tell 6,000 friends."*

All in a heartbeat.

And you can't always predict what will go viral or how it will spin.

From a consumer's standpoint, think about how you enjoy the new level of control we have today. We record TV shows to watch at our convenience and fast-forward through commercials. We view TV online, set up our own virtual newspapers with RSS (Real Simple Syndication) feeds and customize nearly everything.

We have instant movies, 24/7 news, overnight delivery and search engines providing information with immediate results. Twitter and cell phones offer live coverage of events world-wide. We read e-mail at the grocery store, send text messages in the parking lot, and surf the Internet while standing in line.

If we don't like the message, we avoid it.

To twist a phrase, we can turn off, tune out and drop into our own world. Ear buds are ubiquitous, attached to devices that shut out external input and create a private environment.

We expect more and tolerate less.

Not content to believe what we're told, we want to interact. We want input.

We want our voices heard.

And now we have a bullhorn.

GET SOCIAL AND SAVVY

Are you using social media, reading blogs, researching and buying online?

You can't be effective with social media marketing if you've never participated yourself. To be able to relate you have to experience it.

If it's all new to you, don't panic.

Social networking has been around as long as people have. It's a modern term with classic roots, based on human nature.

It's about connections. Getting to know people who have similar interests. Creating a community.

A hundred years ago, community was unavoidable. You needed people. Strong networks grew from trust and mutual dependency. It was a matter of survival.

As people spread out geographically, we became isolated and anonymous.

The Internet came along and made it possible to reestablish relationships, find classmates from elementary school, people you once worked with and friends you haven't seen in years.

It also opened up channels for communication beyond the geographical borders that were impossible a few years ago.

Cancer survivors can reach out to other survivors, new

mothers can join forums where they exchange stories and advice, sports fans can bond - globally.

A sense of community develops between people over common causes and shared interests. It's viral. No borders, no time zones, no barriers.

This fulfills a need people have to interact and exchange experiences. We rely on each other, just as we have done for centuries.

For example, if you move to a new town, how do you find a dentist, doctor or veterinarian?

Chances are you ask around.

If your neighbor raves about their dentist, it carries more weight than a yellow pages ad.

If you've had a great massage, you are likely to suggest that therapist to a friend with aches and pains.

Humans find satisfaction in sharing information. We like to help others.

So if it's been around forever, why is it such a big deal now?

Because the Internet has taken the concept of networking and pumped it up. You can talk with people all over the world and broadcast your opinion to anyone who wishes to hear it.

You can join organizations, attend interactive seminars and

tell the world your thoughts.

You can tweet and blog and comment globally.

All without leaving your home or office.

It's time to jump in, if you haven't already. There are a number of ways to connect to other people where you can reach out, share your knowledge and establish your expertise.

Here are some painless ways to get into the social media stream, starting with those I think will be the least intimidating for a newbie.

Yahoo groups and other discussion groups

A discussion group is a collection of like-minded people who want to share information and exchange opinions. You can join and listen and learn, then contribute when you have something to say.

You get to know the people in your group by their comments and conversations, the way you would in a face-to-face situation.

Anyone can start a group and membership criteria is set by the list owner. E-mail discussion groups are a membership based collection of people with similar interests. There are many e-mail discussion groups in addition to Yahoo, such as AWeber, ListServ and Google (contact info on this on website).

They've been around a long time. I still belong to some I joined a dozen years ago.

You can begin by searching for groups that interest you. I'll use Yahoo's group as an example, but they all function in a similar way.

Go to the Yahoo group page and there's a box to search for groups by interests. A list of active groups appears with information on how many members they have, how recently they've been active, if they are public or by membership only and how long ago they were created.

If you find one you like, click on *"Join this Group"* and become a part of the online community.

Subscribe to Blogs

The best way to learn what works and what doesn't on the Internet is to participate as a consumer. One of the easiest ways to do this is by subscribing to blogs.

Learning about how blogs work and seeing for yourself what you find interesting and worth reading is excellent preparation for your own content-building later on.

Blogs, the term coming from the words *"web"* and *"log"*, originated as an online diary of sorts where individuals would write, or post, their thoughts and activities.

Because it's easy for a non-technical person to use, it's evolved into a valuable business tool, where a person can post, or update, information and create a way for consumers to interact with the company.

You can find blogs by looking for people you think are interesting and seeing if they have a blog.

There are many ways to find blogs you might like, and one is to read the posts in the discussion groups you have now joined. People usually have their website or blog listed in their signature line, and if you like what they have to say, go check out their site.

You can always simply search. Google has a blog search, as does Best of the Web Blog Directory, IceRocket.com and others. I have a list of links in the Resources section of my website.

As you become more comfortable, visit StumbleUpon, Reddit and Tumblr or check directories like Alltop, Technorati and Blog Catalog. There are also services that aggregate information such as Paper.li and Utopic.

You don't need to understand them all right now. As you get familiar with digital marketing, they'll make more sense.

At this point the goal is to get you involved. Once you select a few blogs you find interesting, you'll also find links in the posts and from comments that can lead you to other interesting blogs. The next step is to subscribe, so you get the information regularly.

There's usually two ways to subscribe: by e-mail or by RSS

feed. E-mail is self-explanatory. You sign up and receive an e-mail every time the person posts. This can get out of hand if you subscribe to five, ten or fifty blogs. Managing your inbox becomes a challenge.

What if you could funnel all these updates into an easy-to-read format where you can skim them and read what interests you? The answer to that is RSS feeds. RSS, or Real Simple Syndication, is akin to building your own newspaper page.

When you subscribe to an RSS feed, the blog automatically sends updates to your page and you can read everything there. There are dozens of feed systems, such as Bloglines, Technorati, FeedReader, NewsIsFree, My Yahoo! and Google.

You may want to try a few of the RSS Readers to see what format you prefer. Once you have your "newspaper" page set up, you can add RSS feeds for the blogs you like and review them at your convenience.

Subscribe to several blogs on a variety of topics. This will give you a chance to see how they work, which ones appeal to you, what makes them readable and interesting. This is important information for when you start your own.

When you find blogs you enjoy, participate by commenting. Your comments should be meaningful, reflecting the fact that you've read the post and have something worthwhile to say.

You might notice people leaving comments such as, *"Great post! Thanks for writing it."* This is usually followed by a blatant reference to their own blog or business site.

Commenting that way will not bring respect or further your cause, because it's self-serving.

However, sincere honest comments are appreciated and can start some great conversations, which can lead to additional opportunities and beneficial exposure.

Visit Other Websites

Use the Internet to do research, shop, review, learn.
Visit a variety of websites and look at them like a marketer.

What catches your eye?

How is the purchasing experience? Can you get in touch with a person?

You can learn a lot from seeing how other businesses present themselves. If they are doing something that you think is innovative or well done, drop them an e-mail and tell them.

Positive connections can yield unexpected benefits.

This can begin a dialogue that could lead to future collaboration or even joint marketing efforts. Cooperation is a sensible way to make limited resources go farther.

Positioning

Traditional interruptive marketing is out of style.

Consumers are flexing their power. They want information, they want answers and dialog, they want to share experiences.

Instead of pushing the message at them, the way businesses have done in the past, it's about solutions, shared knowledge and support, bringing customers in and building trust.

This trend is only going to increase.

Are you positioned well to take advantage of the opportunities?

If you're a Skinny Budget Marketer, you're in the right place at the right time.

There are abundant and affordable opportunities to promote your products and services and build loyal customers. This is due, in large part, to the Internet.

Without spending a bucket-load of money, you can educate, create interest and build credibility so clients come to you.

Seth Godin calls it *"permission marketing"*. On his blog, he says *"Permission marketing is the privilege (not the right) of delivering anticipated, personal and relevant messages to people who actually want to get them."*

What a concept.

He compares it to dating, where you grant permission as the relationship and trust increases.

He explains that if you have real permission, then when you don't show up, or your newsletter doesn't arrive on time, people notice.

They miss you because *they wanted to hear from you.*

It's not hard-sell, but it is hard.

While it takes less money, sometimes no money, to implement these new methods, it takes a greater time commitment and a lot of thought to make them effective. **Plan to devote 1-2 hours a week to your marketing, just like you do with any other necessary task.**

Today's business model recognizes that the business doesn't decide what works, the consumer does, and the business responds accordingly.

Savvy companies listen, interact and include their customers in ways that didn't previously exist.

The interaction opens the door to conversation. You can talk to your best resource, your customer, and get answers.

If you aren't selling enough of your product or service, go to the people who are buying and ask them why they buy and how they are using your product.

Ask them what it is about your service that keeps bringing them back. You might discover it's different than what you'd been assuming. At the least, you'll get insight into what people are really doing with your product or getting from your service.

Use this information to do a better job of positioning your product or service. Build on your success with those who already like you and trust you.

Much is made of the relationship aspect of social media. It's not a secret formula. Customer relationships develop in the same way as personal ones always have.

The initial contact, a search for common ground, an exchange of information, increasing trust, and finally a point where you feel secure with each other.

The process unfolds over hours, days, weeks - sometimes even months or years.

The barriers between businesses and their customers are crumbling, but what hasn't changed is the consideration and conduct that form lasting relationships.

The strength of the relationship increases with time, sharing, mutual trust and experience. And just like personal relationships, some will work out, some won't. Some people will be around a long time, others won't.

When we value our clients, provide an excellent product or service, educate and support them, they tell their friends, and our business grows.

What's changed is the rate that communication can spread.

Word of mouth can ignite with lightening speed and take off like a brush fire, burning fast, hot and indiscriminately.

It can catch you by surprise.

Business owners I talk to worry about how to handle unfavorable attention. I think the following account is helpful.

Grand Forks, North Dakota, a town of about 55,000 residents, had a new restaurant and Marilyn Hagerty, the 85-year-old columnist for the *EatBeat*, visited the new Olive Garden and wrote a review, something she'd been doing for decades.

Someone thought it was amusing and shared it.

Her column got more than 200,000 views online, showed up over 20,000 times on Facebook and over 14,000 times on Twitter. Marilyn was not only surprised, she was so unfamiliar with technology, that when informed she'd gone "viral", she had to ask what it meant.

She was flooded with phone calls for interviews. According to her son, who wrote an article in the Wall Street Journal about his mom's sudden fame, the questions most people asked were if she was for real and how she felt about being mocked in cyberspace.

It turns out she really didn't care all that much. She had things to do and didn't plan to read the stuff that was being said about her. She handled the sudden attention with grace and dignity.

And guess what? That reaction endeared her to many and she got support from unexpected places.

Anthony Bourdain, best known for his culinary and cultural knowledge, tweeted *"Very much enjoying watching Internet sensation Marilyn Hagerty triumph over the snarkologists (myself included)."*

Towards her detractors, Marilyn's position was nonchalant.

When the story took off, she was already working on another column about a totally different subject and *"did not have time to twit over whether some self-styled food expert likes, or does not like, my column."*

She didn't ignore the hoopla, but she didn't become combative.

Because of that, she garnered respect.

Marilyn's story illustrates that even today, given the velocity of information broadcasting, the best practices employ classic principles.

That means that, just like Marilyn, you probably already know the basics.

Some of the hot discussion topics surrounding new media include transparency, honesty, not tricking people, offering something before asking for something, respecting your audience, thinking of their needs and problems before yours, caring... Sounds a lot like the Golden Rule.

The Golden Rule, sometimes called *"the ethic of reciprocity,"* has been traced as far back as Confucius' time in 551 B.C.

The principle, simply stated: *"One should treat others as one would like others to treat oneself."*

Still good advice.

It's true that now that consumers have a whole new level of control and input, they want a new level of response and resolution.

This can be scary for a business owner, but keep Marilyn in mind. If she can handle it, you can, too.

FORMULATING YOUR STRATEGY

Marketing and sales both fuel a healthy business, and are often used interchangeably, but they are distinctly different.

Marketing cultivates interest, educates consumers and generates leads.

Sales convert interest into action and completes the purchasing cycle.

Fantastic marketing won't increase your bottom line unless it's backed up with an effective sales process. Make sure you have good procedures in place to turn your prospects into purchasers.

Your marketing strategy identifies your marketing objectives, or what you want to accomplish, which in turn determines your tactics. Tactics are things like blogging, Facebook, Twitter and the like.

In this book, I'm defining tactics as action, and strategy as planning.

The planning has to be in place before you can decide on the action. It seems obvious when you read it, but this is where people often go wrong.

They implement the tactic, like signing up for Facebook, before they have a strategy. They end up with a fan page, but no idea why or what to do with it.

The other tactical mistake is to jump into the latest craze to the exclusion of all else.

Your choice of tactics is broad and varied. New things are fun, but the old ones can pay off as well.

The tactics you choose should be those that get the results your want and accomplish your strategic goals in an integrated and productive way.

Digital marketing is an important part of the Skinny Budget

Marketer's toolbox, but there are plenty of worthwhile old-school techniques that work together with digital marketing to get you the results you want.

Don't get discouraged by the endless choices and new technology that spring up daily in digital marketing. It's true that it takes time to learn how to use and maintain social media. Approach it like any other task: Figure out what you want to accomplish and you'll be able to pick the best tools.

Stay focused on the question: Will this help your business?

Marketing and advertising are highly competitive, primarily because they're so subjective. Big corporations are constantly hiring and firing ad agencies, hoping each time to find one that can see into the future and design campaigns that never disappoint.

That might be possible if everyone was identical, but even using demographics, the study of statistical characteristics of a population and particular groups within it, consumers are not easily categorized.

That's the challenge for business people.

It's hard to create a winner every time. Even the professionals produce their share of failures. Consider the Super Bowl commercials. There are winners and losers, but which are which?

I might like the one you hate and you might love the one I loathe. That's part of the fun every year - discussing what we think works. And advertisers spend millions gambling that we'll remember their product.

Marketing is trial and error. You're always testing, keeping what works and replacing what doesn't. It's part of the process.

To be well-positioned, you need to know what your business is, who your customer is and what you have to offer.

WHAT IS YOUR BUSINESS?

People are driven by three desires: to satisfy a basic need, to solve a problem or to make themselves feel good. Which of these three or which combination of these does your product or service achieve?

Determining the market viability of your business means asking a few qualifying questions.

Are there enough people who what this product or service? Are they willing to pay for it?

Are all their needs currently being met or is there an opportunity to offer something unique?

Is there a cost-effective way to reach the market?

Where does your idea fit?

Take a piece of paper and along the left side write "exclusive" and along the bottom write "desirable". In this grid, the top left area would be for something that's very exclusive, possibly available only through you, but not very desirable. It's something people aren't eager to have.

The bottom left would be something that's commonly available, not exclusive at all, but again, not desirable.

The bottom right would be something that's commonly available but in demand, something people want.

The top right would be something that people want, which is also exclusive, available primarily through you.

Where does your product or service fall in this diagram?

If it's in the top left, your challenge is to create a desire for this product or service. Perhaps consumers simply don't understand why they need it.

If in the bottom left, you challenges are steep. If you are here, you might want to reconsider your offering.

In the bottom right, you're going to have a lot of others vying for the same market. This usually leads to price competition, a business-killing practice.

The position you want to have is the top right - a product or service people want and one that you can provide using your unique qualifications.

Let's walk through an example.

Perhaps you've always dreamed of owning a pet store. That's

fine, but unless you want to pour buckets of money into it to keep it going, you'll want to begin by figuring out if there's a need for a pet store in your area.

Are there potential customers who have a problem your pet store can solve?

Researching this, you discover that people want to buy tropical fish. In fact, the market for tropical fish is huge in your town.

The next step is to determine if there are other companies selling tropical fish. Who are they? How are they doing it?

What if there are no other places selling tropical fish in your town?

What does that tell you?

It should tell you to dig deeper.

Why? Maybe delivery is impossible and there's no way to get healthy fish on a consistent basis. Or zoning prohibits fish stores in any location that would be attractive.

This might have discouraged others, but you know of potential solutions. You can tackle the obstacles and overcome them before you launch your business.

Occasionally, there might not be a business like the one you want to begin because there is no market, or there are obstacles too big to conquer. You want to know this now, rather than later when you've invested your life savings.

However, let's say there are two other fish stores. That doesn't need to dismay you. If they are doing well, it should encourage you, because there is a market and it is doable.

Additionally, instead of competitors being enemies, there might be opportunities to work together at some point.
The next step is to determine what you bring to the table.

You decided on this business for a reason. You have ability, knowledge or experience others don't have. You might have greater enthusiasm or passion than the other guy. Maybe your strength is follow-through or in managing details.

Whatever it is that makes you different plays a big role in creating your brand and planning your marketing strategy.

It's often referred to as a Unique Selling Proposition or Unique Sales Point (USP), which I described earlier when I gave my unique qualifications. It's what sets you apart from your competition, what provides a clear benefit to your customer.

It's not enough that you are offering the product or service. Certainly you are an individual, and unique on that basis, but what value does that have for your client?

If you are telling people you're unique because you *care about people*" or you take them to coffee, that's not enough.

If your competitors can say the same thing, then it's not very unique.

You care about people - great - how do you demonstrate it?

The ways you show your concern are qualities that set you apart.

I developed my USP through trial and error. Real-life testing. I talked to people and asked them what they wanted and looked for how that matched up with my talents and skills.

They wanted to understand and not be made to feel stupid. They wanted to deal with someone who had experience with their business challenges, who knew how to work with limited capital, who had practical skills. They didn't want to be told, they wanted to be heard.

I found that my teaching and writing background helps me explain concepts in a way that make sense. My experience with traditional marketing, my background running small businesses, my curiosity and skepticism give me common ground with company owners.

I also relate to a demographic that often feels overlooked or disregarded in the social media madness.

We share the same goals for their business.

Refine your USP by thinking like your client. Why do they buy your product or service? What are the reasons behind the obvious? If you were on a panel with five other people in your industry, what could you offer that's exceptional and distinct?

Do you know what they're really looking for?

Charles Revson, founder of the Revlon cosmetics empire,

understood his customers. Although his products were lipstick and eye shadow, what he was selling was the belief that these things would make a difference in their lives.

What he really sold was *hope.*

Hope, in the form of an everyday product.

What are you really selling?

Returning to our fish story. Research shows that fish have a calming effect on people. Children settle down when there is a tropical fish tank in the classroom. Patients in waiting rooms are more relaxed when gazing at fish swimming in a tank.

Maybe as the owner of our hypothetical fish store you can create aquatic environments that enhance this effect and your niche, your USP, is that you *sell peace of mind in a chaotic world.*

By finding your niche, you're able to focus on the segment of consumers who give you majority of your business.

This is the genesis of your marketing strategy - getting clear about your business. What it is, your target market and what success looks like to you.

Here's an exercise I often use. Fill in the blanks.

I do _____ for _____ so they can _____.

You don't have to use these exact words, but what you're after is:

    1- the essence of what you do,
    2- the person you do it for and
    3- how it changes things for them

This exercises helps you get to the core ideas about your business.

Distilling the description down to a few words is powerful. More words do not a better description make.

In fact, several business and marketing pundits advocate brevity across the board.

Seth Godin warns that people are going to start complaining about things being too long, that no one will be upset if it's too short, but he cautions that *"Shorter, though, doesn't mean less responsibility, less insight or less power. It means less fluff and less hiding."*

Guy Kawasaki recommends writing a 3-4 word mantra that captures the essence of your company. Not the public tag line, rather it's the internal description that inspires and defines the company for you or the employees.

He cites Nike, whose customer slogan is *"Just Do It"*. Kawasaki suggests the mantra should be *"Authentic Athletic Performance"*, because that's what the company is to the employee - authentic athletic performance.

Kawasaki's own mantra is *Empowering Entrepreneurs.*

What is yours?

WHO IS YOUR CUSTOMER

Skinny Budget Marketers know their customers. To give them a personal identity, you can create an archetype of your primary customer. An archetype is a typical example, or profile.

Begin by asking yourself, *who is your target customer?*

Hint: it's not everybody, everyone with skin or those with a pulse. No matter how great your product or service is, not everyone is a potential client.

That's good news, though.

The 80/20 rule reminds us that 80 percent of the business comes from 20 percent of the people. It's much easier to find and communicate with 20 percent than 100 percent, and more effective, too. We want to identify that 20 percent.

List the demographics and psychographics:

> Gender?
> Age?
> Education?
> Where do they live?
> Married? Children?
> Income?

Career or job? Retired?
Lifestyle?
Interests and activities?
Hobbies?
Likes?
Dislikes?
Attitudes and beliefs?
What do they worry about?
What keeps them up at night?

If you have several prime customers, develop an archetype for each one. Name them so you can get to know your customer profile.

This takes your target market out of the theoretical and personifies it.

One of my primary archetypes is Mary, the Multitasking Entrepreneur. She's 48, single, educated and reasonably ambitious.

She sees technology as a necessary evil. She prefers to hire someone else to implement her marketing, but she wants to be informed.

She's upbeat, clever and tired of being ignored.

I like Mary, and I wonder what she's up to.

What's her biggest problem today? What does she need that would make her life, her business, easier?

Where does she get the information she uses to make her buying decisions? Does she read newspapers and magazines? Watch TV? Surf the Internet? Spend time on Facebook? Pinterest? Twitter?

I can fill in the answers to these questions because Mary is not imaginary to me, she's a real person, with real dreams and challenges that I can help her with.

What about your archetype?

There is a lot of social media demographic information available online, and you can use it to match your archetype to the social media they are most likely to use. Here again, because it changes so much, I won't list the links here, but I've included some on my website under Resources.

How does this information help you? At this point in time, 82 percent of Pinterest users are women, compared to 59 percent for Twitter, 57 percent for Facebook and just 29 percent for Google+.

LinkedIn has the highest educated demographic, twice as many with degrees as Facebook or Twitter. Three out of four people on LinkedIn are using it for business.

Where will I find Mary?

She might be on all of them, but I have to focus on a manageable number.

My top two picks for her would be LinkedIn and Pinterest.

Now it's your turn.

Where does your archetype go for information and recommendations? Do they use Facebook? Twitter? Where do they hang out? At home? Work? Ski hills? Farmer's markets?

Wherever it is, you need to be there.

In order of most likely to least likely, make a list of places, online or in the physical world, where you think you'll find your archetype. Then pick the top two.

If you're stumped about where your primary customer hangs out is - ask them.

If you don't want to do it face-to-face, use surveys, comment cards, or delegate it.

Your current customers, who already do business with you can be a gold mine of information about what your ideal clients want and need from your business.

WHAT DEFINES SUCCESS?

This is different for everyone.

Despite the trend to connect success with financial prosperity, money is not the definition of success.

I prefer this definition: *"Success is the outcome of an undertaking, specified as achieving its aims."*

Your desired outcome is the definition of what success means to you.

I work with a lot of writers. For some, success is completing a manuscript. For others, it's publication. Some want to see their books in libraries, or in a bookstore, or on the best-seller list.

Some want a comfortable income and a modest life, while others want to be interviewed on the major TV networks. Some want to write and produce a play, others want to write a movie script.

Yet all are writers. And each goal is a legitimate measurement of success - because success is defined by the individual.

However, the methods, strategy and tactics will differ widely, because the desired outcomes are so different.

In his book, *7 Habits of Highly Effective People,* Steven Covey advised to begin with the end in mind, and suggested readers write their obituary.

An obit is a summary of the accomplishments of a person's life. If you wrote your own, it would include what you wanted to be remembered for, what you were proud of, what you achieved.

Instead of writing about your life, you can write the obituary for your business. What do you want your business legacy to be?

Ask yourself: To whom did my business make a difference? What did people who used my product or service have to say? How do I know I succeeded?

It's just another way to look at your business goals and the more you know, the better your chance of success.

Now you know what you do, who your target customer is and your desired outcome.

What stands between you and that outcome?

Money? Knowledge? Competition?

Write down the things you need to acquire, learn or achieve in order to reach success, then list the steps to accomplish that. You can apply for financing, take classes, size up your competition and find your niche.

If you want to get specific with this examination, you can take it to the next level with the Strengths, Weaknesses/Limitations, Opportunities, and Threats (SWOT) Analysis, a strategic planning tool every business should be familiar with and use periodically.

Don't be intimidated, it's easy to do. Take a sheet of paper and divide it into quadrants, label each one with one of these four headings: Strengths, Weaknesses, Opportunities and Threats.

Under **Strengths**, include things like USP, your resources, capabilities, knowledge, experience, value, processes.

Weaknesses are training you need but don't yet have, financial shortfalls, personnel problems, inventory or production issues.

Opportunities would be new products or services, partnerships, competitor vulnerabilities, new USPs.

Threats are legislative or government burdens, changing consumer demand, transitional staff, economy.

This gives you a clear picture of how your business is positioned for success and what areas to address.

A SWOT analysis is an excellent assessment to use to stay aware of the internal and external influences on your business.

Presenting

Presenting is all about how your business appears to the world.

In the same way that a brick and mortar location was once the measure of legitimacy, a website is crucial to your online credibility.

A user-friendly domain name is equivalent to a choice physical location. It's your little piece of prime property on the Internet.

Often people use their business name for their website address, but there are times when it makes sense to use something else.

Let's say Joe has a business called Joe's Mountain Bike Repair and Sales Shop. The name is long. When it appears as a web address, it boggles the mind.

Joesmountainbikerepairandsalesshop.com

Even when each word is capitalized to enhance readability the phrase is still daunting.

JoesMountainBikeRepairandSalesShop.com

That's not good.

Joe needs an Internet address that's easy for people to understand and remember. To accomplish that, he might want to find a domain name such as JoesBikes.com, BikeRepair.com, or BikeSales.com.

If you see JoesBikes.com on a billboard as you zip down the highway, you can remember it, at least for as long as it takes to get in front of a computer to look it up. It's simple and logical, which makes it easy.

But what if a simple domain name isn't available? What's the next option?

Even though you can choose extensions such as .biz, .us, .info, .me and others, try to get a primary domain name that's a .com. People still think of .com when they think of websites, so it will be to your advantage to find a .com that works.

So if shorter is better, what if Joe used the first letters of the entire name – jmbrass.com?

It's short – but what does it communicate? It looks like J M Brass, which has nothing to do with Joe's bike business, and won't help anyone find him.

Joe needs to get creative. He needs to call in his friends and try out ideas.

Which one or ones will make the most sense to people when they see it on a business card, a signature line or a tee-shirt?

Joe narrows it down to two options: GoBikes.com or

BikeBonanza.com.

He buys them both, because they're cheap and he may not get another chance, if he doesn't act now (there's only one in the world, and anyone can buy it).

If you are juggling two good options, one short but a bit cryptic and the other longer but clearly logical, my vote would be to choose the logical one. Balance the length against the functionality. If you use words that relate to your business not only will it help people identify you, it also helps search engines find you.

Or buy both. You can always let one go later, or you can redirect the weaker one to your site.

I own many domain names. Since there is only one of that exact name available in the world, it makes sense to me to spend a few dollars securing it for a project I have in mind, even if it might be years down the road. If I decide later I don't need it, I can let it expire. But rarely can I get it back.

YOUR WEBSITE

Your website is the nucleus of your business. It's where people go to learn about you or purchase your product or service. It's the storefront, the clearinghouse of information and resources.

It has to be professional and work for you. It's a 24/7 presence, open for business even while you sleep.

You can build your own site or you can hire someone to create it for you. If you want to do it yourself, there are free services out there, but if you're serious about your business, avoid using a free web platform.

If you use a free platform, you are taking a risk. Your "website" is just a section of theirs. The traffic you get boosts their SEO and rankings, and does nothing for you in the long-term. If they disappear, your "site" goes with them.

It makes as much sense as remodeling a rental property. You put in a lot of work and someone else benefits. It's a poor use of your time and money.

Instead, you want to have your own domain name, hosted and owned by you.

Unless you are on a painfully thin budget, consider having your site built by a professional. It's not that it's magic. Given enough time I'm sure you could learn what you need, but since you don't do it every day, it's going to be harder and take longer and still might not be right.

Your time is limited, and it would be wiser to spend it creating good content and building relationships in social media - an ongoing process - instead of trying to master another business.

Hire a trusted expert to build the site and concentrate your efforts on those things that directly benefit from your personal involvement.

If you use an agency or graphic designer, make sure their priorities are in line with your needs. Don't be fooled into thinking a work of art is the same as an effective website. Your designer should understand your business needs and be able to explain how the site can accomplish your goals. In style vs. substance, it's substance that will get results.

Where websites are concerned, it pays to have more than one. Sites that are informational, sites that promote a single product, sites that are landing pages, sites that are instructional increase your exposure on the Internet and target specific needs.

In real estate, for example, you could have an individual property website for each listing, because HomeFinder studies show that 3 million monthly home searches are for the exact address.

Don't limit yourself or your potential to a single site.

You want a site, or sites, you can keep current without complications, since managing your content is important.

I recommend finding someone who can build you an optimized WordPress self-hosted site. It's what I use exclusively for my clients.

Building from the ground up gives you the ability to incorporate the elements that are important.

But what if you already have a site?

Give it a checkup.

Look at it through a stranger's eyes. Can someone who doesn't know you tell what your site is about in 10 seconds?

That's how long people spend deciding if they are going to stay on a site or move on. If they can't figure out what you're about, you need to revise your presentation.

Make sure it's instantly apparent what your business, service or purpose is.

Is there a call to action? Is there a clear path to the next step?

Too many sites either have multiple calls to action or none at all. You spend time and money driving traffic to your site - what do you want them to do when then get there? Is it obvious? Does it serve your business?

People skim on the Internet. They multi-task. Don't make it difficult for them to understand what you do or how you can help them.

And don't play hide-and-seek with your contact information.

Have a Contact tab in an obvious place. As you visit websites in your research, where do you instinctively look for contact information?

Most people look for a Contact tab or go to the bottom to find it. If your page is too long, your tabs are in a weird place or you eliminate this information because it doesn't look pretty, you are putting style over substance and forgetting the purpose of your site.

The purpose of your site is to get business. To get business, people have to know how to reach you.

What about information? Do you address the common questions people have about your product or service?

What should you include? If you have people asking you the same questions over and over, you might want to put those answers on your site.

This doesn't mean you need to answer every conceivable question - some are better handled in personal conversation - but you want to provide enough information to engage them and demonstrate your knowledge.

For every person who contacts you because they couldn't find answers, just as many give up. The goal is to keep them engaged with you.

Is your information current? Do the links work? If your website never changes, has outdated references and stale material, you're training people to ignore you.

Does your site make it inviting for consumers to do business with you? How can it be improved to make it even easier?

By decreasing friction.

Friction, as it's used in marketing, is anything that makes it difficult for your client to do business with you. The less friction, the more business you get.

Think about Amazon. They make it simple to buy - 1-click - and offer Prime two-day shipping delivered to your door. They suggest products you might like based on previous searches.

They inform you about items you might want that have been discounted. They show you what other people bought who were looking at what you were looking at. They allow you, for better or for worse, to comment on your experience with the product and you can read the comments of others.

It's easy. So easy.

Zappos is another online seller who has built a reputation for being wonderful company. Their success can be traced to putting people before profits - and the result is customers love them and they've been consistently rated as one of the best places to work. At Zappos you can talk to a real person and be treated like you matter.

The good news is, whether you are a big company or small one, you can duplicate these successful practices and reap the benefits.

CHECK OUT YOUR COMPETITOR'S WEBSITES

What's the first thing you notice? What's the message? Can you find what you're looking for, is it easy to navigate, is the information accessible and does it answer your questions?

Look at what they are doing right and where they could improve. Now look at your site again. What can you do to make it better?

An effective website helps the consumer make the decision to buy your product or service. It supports and reinforces the other advertising you do, and saves money because your paid ads can be brief and concise.

Paid ads can send them to the site for in-depth information, where you have the space to tell the whole story and can answer questions.

For example, if you sell energy efficient windows, you can run an ad offering a special price, and direct people to the website to find out how long you've been in business, why your windows are high quality and what your selection looks like.

Make sure there's an actual person available to respond to customer inquiries. Don't hide behind an impersonal maze of anonymous clicks, automated responses or someone reading a script in a boiler room.

Consumers are hungry to speak with a real person who knows the business and works to find solutions for them.

Big companies are trying to figure out how to increase the personal touch. As a small business, you have an advantage. Small companies are experts on individualized service.

CONTENT

Content is like air - vital to your business survival.

But not just any content. It has to be relevant, genuinely useful and interesting.

Recycled, irrelevant, meaningless words are not going to do the job. Automated blogging tools and mass-produced content just clog up cyberspace with garbage.

Like smog, it pollutes, and makes us desperate to find clean, fresh air to sustain us.

Doing business with companies that advertise that they can provide content with no effort on your part can also get you in trouble with copyright violations, credibility and blacklisting.

On the other hand, creating your own quality content can improve your search engine rankings, drive traffic to your website, and help nurture existing clients.

So, what is content?

I define it as *that which you produce and share.*

It's information. It can vary in topic, scope, specifics and delivery, but when information is distributed to an audience, it's content.

If you take the time to create great original content, you can spin it off in a dozen different ways.

Some include:

Articles
Blogging
Books
Events
Infographics
Newsletters
News Releases
Podcasts
Speaking/Presentations
Videos
Webinars/Online Conferences
Website
White Papers

There are many ways to use excellent content.

CONTENT STRATEGY

Three things make up your content strategy:

KNOW your audience
KNOW your purpose
KNOW your message

Your Audience

How well your content works depends on how well you know your customer and their needs.

Content, like social media channels, should be guided by your target market.

As you begin blogging and get feedback you might be surprised at what your audience perceives as valuable.

It can change the focus of your posts. It could even change the purpose of your site. Keep an open mind and pay attention to the conversations, and you could discover a lucrative niche you hadn't even realized existed.

Does your target market watch videos? Listen to podcasts? Do they want infographics or surveys? Do they prefer to read text? View photos?

As a writer, I believe content should include text in the mix. Personally I don't gravitate to videos or podcasts first because they are time-consuming.

I like to skim, and if the content looks promising, I'll dive in. If not, I've only wasted a few minutes. I think a lot of consumers are like me, so I always use written words, and enhance with garnishes like video, podcasting and the like.

Sonia Simone says, *"Give your audience a range of formats and observe what works best. Do that and you'll never have to worry about falling prey to profit-killing fads."*

If you're fascinated by shiny new channels, don't let your infatuation lead you astray. It's what your customers are fascinated with that will lead them to your business.

While you're considering the format of your content, it's also important to think about where your target market is in the buying cycle.

Are they in the beginning stages, just realizing they might need your product or service? Maybe they're past that and are now researching options. Once they have enough information, they'll start narrowing down their choices so they can make a decision. Finally, they're ready to do business with you and purchase.

But it doesn't end there. You need to nurture clients with good service, follow up and loyalty-building content, too.

You'll want to have content for consumers at every stage. Some ideas for each stage might be:

> Thinking - blog posts, social media connections
> Researching - articles, webinars
> Deciding - sampling, tutorials, consultation
> Purchasing - guarantees, testimonials, instructions

By having depth and breadth in your content, you can shorten the sales cycle, establish better relationships and encourage referrals.

In order to achieve the goals you set, it helps to use an editorial calendar. Magazines have been using them for years to organize and plan issues far in advance.

You are a publisher of your own content, and an editorial calendar is a useful tool. Not only to plan your marketing, but to budget the time you will need to accomplish the plan.

Use your editorial calendar to arrange topics and identify issues you want to address in the future. If you decide to have guest bloggers or do interviews, you can stagger them among your own posts.

Once you have a visual plan, you'll see where content might be used in additional ways or tied in with other activities.

You'll also get a feel for where there are holes in your coverage. Aim for balance in the subject matter and the delivery method - text, videos, podcasts, etc. As you proceed, review your most popular posts and analyze why people liked them. Perhaps you need more of these.

Develop a backlog of evergreen material you can use and reframe, or plug in if something falls through on the calendar.

Your Purpose

Want do you want to accomplish?

You can have several different objectives, tailored to different markets. The important thing is to have a purpose for your content so you don't end up wandering all over aimlessly.

Are you launching a new product? Holding an event? Trying to encourage more business during a slow time?

What are you going to do to make this happen?

Is that video of the monkey throwing your thermos into the pond just funny or does it make a point? It's okay to entertain, but even better to entertain and inform.

Are you putting together an infographic because it's fun to do or is there point?

Why will a consumer read, watch or listen to this?

What do you want them to know once they're done?

What do you want them to do once they're done?

Your Message

Your message, and how you deliver it, is a key factor in successful content production.

How do you cut through the confusion?

There's so much noise out there that we'd all go crazy if it wasn't for our Reticula Activating System (RAS). If this system wasn't in place, everything would come through our consciousness with equal importance and we'd collapse under the stress of too much information.

What gets through our RAS?

> Things that are unusual
> Things that threaten us
> Things we value

If it's not one of these three, we forget 95% of what we are exposed to within 72 hours.

You see this implemented in various ways. TV news is one

place where I really notice it. Test it for yourself. Doesn't every story fall into one of those three categories?

They know what makes us pay attention.

That's why valuable content has the potential to get noticed. But what makes it valuable?

The experts out there tell you to write for your target market, but what does that mean?

It's more than just fitting your topic to their needs. If you want your content to transcend the average, then everything you do when promoting your business should be filtered through your customer's eyes. You have to learn to see things from their point of view.

How does that differ from how you are looking at it now?

Instead of thinking about what you are or do, you switch and think about what's in it for your customer.

When you explain your business to people, you probably emphasize the features of your product or service. You're anxious to share just how wonderful they are.

After all, these fabulous features are the things you've come up with to solve a problem. Just like the experts advised.

But that value might not be obvious to the consumer. It might not even exist for them yet, or they might not recognize it as important.

Telling your customer about this terrific feature will be meaningless to them, unless you can explain how it can benefit them.

CONSUMERS BUY BENEFITS

When I began in advertising years ago, we were taught to think of the Feature, the Advantage, and the Benefit (FAB) of every product or service.

Today the Advantage is often left out of the equation, but I find it useful. This three-step process can transition your thinking from being stuck on the Feature to focusing on the Benefit.

This leads to that "ah-ha" moment when a client understands why they might want a feature they'd never even considered.

For example, let's say you're selling a car that comes with a keypad door lock. That's a Feature, but it may have little value to someone who has never had one and cannot see any reason to care.

You can elaborate on how it's got a soft texture, a pleasing color and the style blends with the car's frame, but they'll just walk away.

How do you explain the Benefit? First, by taking the Feature and defining the Advantage.

The Advantage is that you don't need your keys to unlock your car.

Great, but your consumers are still thinking, so what? They don't see what it means to them. They've been using keys or a key fob for years. Why would they even need to unlock their car using buttons?

Drill down a bit more.

The Benefit? Never be locked out of your car again!

Ah-ha!

Everyone's been locked out of their car. Now you've presented a universal Benefit - one that any car owner understands.

Now you've looked at the keypad through the eyes of your customer. The Feature that meant nothing before makes sense now.

I don't suggest you walk your customer through the process of FAB, instead take yourself through it before you ever talk to them, then present them with the Benefit.

You'll no longer feel frustrated when your customer doesn't get it, because if your customer doesn't get it, it's because you haven't done your job. They'll get it when you give them the benefit. They might even take off with the idea and come up with a few keypad benefits important to them.

The keypad is now an indispensable element in their car criteria.

Make it easy for the consumer to understand why your

features are a good thing. Don't make them struggle to figure it out.

It's all about eliminating the friction.

Another example: If I come to your tire business to buy new car tires and you tell me about the quality of the rubber and cut of the tread using industry language, I won't have a clue why I should care.

Can you show me why it matters? Can you help me make the right choice?

Years ago the Michelin Tire Company connected the dots for consumers when they ran an advertising campaign featuring a baby in a tire, experiencing a rainstorm and blustery weather.

The tagline *"...because so much is riding on your tires."*

It was a strong, clear, unambiguous message, and I got it immediately.

I had children, and I loved my family. *I wanted those tires.*

They were the right choice.

I still remember the Michelin baby today and I don't know how long ago I last saw the image.

It made an impact on me.

When I researched it to mention it in this book, I discovered the michelinman.com website is fascinating. Seriously! They answer all kinds of questions about tires in plain English, with a great diagram illustrating a cross-section of a tire and what the layers do.

The information packed into that site tells me Michelin cares about my concerns, and that they're confident that the more I know about tires, the more I'll want Michelins.

This is a great example of using the Internet wisely to connect with people. The site's informative, easy to navigate and addresses my questions. The call to action is clear: *Tire Selector, Find a Tire Dealer.* It's easy to buy the product.

To reinforce the message, a pop up appears:

"Michelin is conducting a survey to find out how you use and interact with our website. If you're willing to participate in a short e-mail survey about your online experience, please enter your information below. We appreciate your input!"

They want feedback.

It's exactly what people are seeking today; information, education and the chance to be heard.

You can offer this, too, using your content.

WHERE DOES YOUR EXCELLENT CONTENT LIVE?

If quality content appeals to consumers and search engines, you want a place to collect and showcase this great stuff you're creating.

You want to be able to build a library of material, and determine how and where to feature it. You can't do this on Facebook, but you can on your own website.

Your website is the hub of your entire marketing strategy, and is the repository for the valuable information you offer.

The most common method of showcasing content is a blog. Long ago it was dismissed as a passing fad used primarily by narcissists, but blogs have evolved, and become essential for anyone who creates content, which should be anyone in business today.

Blogging platforms such as the previously mentioned WordPress.org are being used to replace traditional static websites by people who want a powerful way to have a presence on the Internet.

The benefits are numerous.

The ability to post makes it easy to update your content without having any technical training. You can publish fresh content easily, on your time schedule. It's a great way to keep consumers informed about new releases or products, and provide news tips about your industry.

Frequent and consistent posting builds your audience. Blogging daily is highly effective, but so is blogging weekly.

Depending on your content, goals and audience, you can build loyalty blogging monthly, too, if you deliver excellent content on a consistent basis. This requires a regular commitment of time every week, just like accounting chores.

Blogs are informal and friendly, encouraging interaction and relationships.

Subscriptions increase the attractiveness of blogging. If someone is interested in reading the things you post, they don't have to remember to visit your site every day.
Instead, they can subscribe. This makes it effortless for them to keep up with what you have to say.

Readers can subscribe to your blog posts by signing up to get them delivered to their e-mail or through an RSS feed, the same way you did earlier when you subscribed to blogs that interest you.

Every time you post something new on your blog, your subscriber receives it automatically.

Having this excellent content available on your own website gives you a base from which to broadcast your services and a reason to use social media to funnel interested consumers to the place where they can do business with you.

Promoting

Everything we've done so far comes together to define your marketing strategy.

You've described your product or service, how it fits into the marketplace, what makes it unique, what competition and obstacles you face, who your target customer is, and what content you can create to serve this market and build your business.

Now, how to promote your business? What can you do so people come to your website?

As with a storefront, you can built it, stock it and turn on the lights, but that doesn't mean you'll get traffic.

The occasional lookie-loo might wander by, but in order to get the customers you need, you have get the word out.

Put your web address is on everything you produce, including business cards, letterhead, signs, promotional materials and the product itself.

Don't forget your e-mail signature. If you send 10 e-mails a day, that's 3,650 opportunities to get your website seen.

You also want to be seen online, so make sure your website is attractive to search engines.

WEBSITE SEO

If you aren't familiar with SEO, it stands for Search Engine Optimization. It means doing things that increase the chances your site will be found in the top results of a search.

Google, Yahoo and Bing are the top search engines, but there are others. If you search the term "search engines", you'll get a huge list, including DogPile, AltaVista, Lycos and Ask.

Every search engine has specific criteria for ranking, and it's evolving constantly.

When you use a search engine, you type words describing what you are looking for into the search box. The search engine program indexes documents or web pages and matches the results with the words you typed.

Results come up, usually in the thousands, and the best matches are supposed to be on the first few pages of the Search Engine Results Page (SERP). That's the place to be, as people don't often go past the first several pages to read the results.

Ever since search engines came along, people have tried to figure out how to manipulate these results to make specific sites come up on the first page every time.

They study the algorithms, or processes, that search engines use to rank websites.

Search engines don't want people to know exactly how they determine rankings. Why? If people figure out the formula, they can skew the results and that hurts the credibility of the search engine.

If you don't get good, reliable results from Google, for example, you'll use Yahoo, or another one.

In order remain relevant, they have to stay ahead of the game and consistently deliver valuable information.

Search engines love original, meaningful content and one of the ways they identify and index pages is through content keywords, matching them to what's typed in the search bar.

If these words are in your content, they can help you get found.

When people knew this, Search Engine Optimization (SEO) became the obsession of anyone with a website. Businesses promising SEO miracles bloomed like wildflowers.

It didn't take long for the unscrupulous to start cramming keywords into unrelated content in order to distort results, forcing search engines to constantly reevaluate how they determine results to thwart manipulators.

SEO is an on-going job, one that's never done. Most small businesses don't have the time nor the expertise to chase ranking, but there are things you can do to improve your SEO.

It comes back to content. You can leverage the effect of great content using social media and inbound links.

Inbound links, also called back links or incoming links, are when other sites link to yours.

Inbound links accomplish two things.

One, search engines conclude you are trustworthy and valuable when they see other sites link to yours.

Secondly, consumers conclude the same thing. If a website they like and respect contains a link to your product or service, the good feelings carry over to you, the way a personal referral might.

In addition, since they are usually on a site about a topic already interesting to them, you've connected with your target market and increased the chances of a business relationship.

For example, if a consumer is searching for information about bikes, and reading about trails in their area and comes across a link to Joe's repair shop, they might become a customer. Their interest is already established.

Social media can get you links like this and build credibility, too.

Every time you interact with someone, in the physical world or online, you represent your business. When you're asked for advice or are involved in a discussion, you are building relationships, for better or worse.

Social media gives you a chance to demonstrate your expertise in a non-pushy, supportive way and make a good impression.

If you offer advice people like, they'll link to your blog or website. This is an endorsement, and is priceless.

Everything indicates original content and authentic connections are only going to become more important.

At a recent South by Southwest (SXSW) session, Google's Matt Cutts made waves when he was reported as saying that Google is tweaking the rankings to level the SEO playing field.

According to reports, Google is targeting over-optimization, because they want to discourage those SEO specialists who optimize *at the expense of quality* and encourage those who are producing outstanding content and sites.

Too many keywords and too many links raise red flags for search engines. These techniques have long been staples for optimizers-for-hire, so it will certainly shake up the SEO world if they start penalizing the practice. As this goes to press, speculation is rampant.

Regardless, I'm confident this truth will endure: *One of the best ways to improve your on-site SEO is to have frequently updated, quality content sprinkled with a prudent use of keywords.*

There are no tricks, shortcuts or faking it.

CATEGORIZING YOUR TACTICS - PEOM

There are a lot of tactics to choose from, and you want to have a plan to make sure they work together.

You can sort the different media using the PEOM system so you're not haphazard in how you apply them.

WHAT IS PEOM?

Marketing media is classified into three categories: Paid, Earned and Owned Media (PEOM).

Sorting them is useful, but don't get too bogged down in the categorizing. This exercise is for your benefit, so you can see how you're allocating your promotional efforts. Assign the media to the category that seems to fit best, then put together your promotional plan.

It's the concept behind it that's important - integrating media to accomplish synergy, achieving greater results than any could alone.

Here's the breakdown of the categories.

Paid media is exactly that - you pay for it. It includes display ads, banner ads, pay per click search ads (PPC), sponsorships. An ad in the newspaper, or a magazine. A billboard.

The benefits of paid media is that you control when and where it appears. It's fast, you don't have to wait for your message to disseminate. The drawback is it costs money, often a lot of money, and strains the skinny budget.

The takeaway is that you want to use paid media carefully and as part of a plan. It makes a nice pairing with social media or owned media - in other words, you can use a Facebook ad to highlight your store's grand opening or a special promotion, driving people to your business location or website and reinforcing your Facebook fan page.

Together, earned and owned media can make your paid media investment go farther and be more effective.

Earned media is the media you get from your efforts, your reputation and your interactions. It's the spin-off we've always had, just magnified by the ability of social media to spread the word. As mentioned previously, if you had bad service 20 years ago, you told your friends. Today you can tell the world.

People love to talk, they love to be experts and critics. Social media has made this effortless. Zealous fans promote your product or service every chance they get.

The upside is minimal cost. A handful of people who love your product or service can speak to thousands. These people have great credibility because they are a third party, with nothing to gain by endorsing you.

The downside is people are fickle. If they turn on you, that same broadcast blessing can become a curse. You have no control. You cannot, should not, try to manipulate the conversation.

What you can do is show your best side, communicate, fix the problem if you can, offer help when appropriate and maintain integrity - remember Marilyn.

The takeaway is that word of mouth, and earned media, is influential and here to stay. Keep that in mind and learn to handle yourself within it. Not everyone is going to love you. We found that out in grade school but hopefully we also accepted that it's okay.

Owned media is what belongs to you, in relation to your business. Your website is owned, your newsletters are owned.

Content is a big component of owned media, and as we go on, you'll see how content is a major factor in your marketing success.

The pluses of owned media are that you have control and you can provide real value to your market, in effect creating your own channel of information and knowledge. This builds credibility, you can influence your targeted markets, encourage conversations and nurture your earned media.

It amplifies your paid media efforts.

Figuring out how to use your media channels together will put you ahead of the pack.

Ted Kohnen, of Stein + Partners brand activation (SPBA) says it's a game-changing force: *"PEO is the new SEO - there's a strategy to it, a formula and a lot of hard work. And when it comes together, it really pays off, sustainably, over the long term."*

PROMOTING WITH SOCIAL MEDIA

Social media can increase brand awareness by expanding your reach, build sales by getting consumers into the buying cycle, and reinforce client loyalty by engaging and providing support.

It can drive traffic to your site, your events, trade shows and presentations and improve your search engine rankings.

Through social media connections you can better understand your clients, improve customer service, discover new product ideas and create a referral base.

But social media activity comes after content and website development.

Earned and paid media exists to drive people to your site or your physical location, where they can make a buying decision. You want to invest the bulk of your time ensuring that your product, service and business is sound.

The hub of your business should be where you have the control. That's on your owned media - your website.

FIVE FACTS ABOUT SOCIAL MEDIA

ONE: Social media is not just another advertising channel - pushy product messages don't work.

TWO: You are not going to figure it out without doing it. In some ways, it's a new world. The terminology and customs of the various social media sites are akin to visiting a foreign country.

THREE: Change is the norm. Social media is perpetually

evolving, so what works for you today might not work next week.

This can be discouraging to a small to mid-sized business, but it reinforces the reasons to limit your social media channels to a manageable number. Remember, marketing, especially in social media, requires a scientific approach - testing, evaluating and refining. The media itself could change, and if it becomes too time-consuming to try to adapt, you might want to reevaluate.

FOUR: It takes time. Results are not instant. You cannot force things to happen immediately. Be patient and consistent.

FIVE: You don't need to have relationships with everyone out there - the 80/20 rule applies. Focus on your niche market.

Don't get caught up in the competition of who has the most friends, followers and fans. Numbers don't automatically equal success.

Tom Watson said, "*If you don't genuinely like your customers, chances are they won't buy.*"

How are you going to like them if you don't know them? How are you going to know them if you see them simply as escalating numbers?

If you avoid business socials and meet-and-greets because you think they're an agonizing waste of time, you might not have the temperament for social media.

Or maybe you can try this - define your niche and focus on it. Keep the number of connections reasonable so you can relate in meaningful ways, focused on individuals.

If nothing else, you might want to delegate. Whoever represents you on social media or at social events should project the qualities you value.

Here are four of the most popular social media channels, as of this moment, but keep in mind that new ones appear regularly.

The leaders are Facebook, Twitter and LinkedIn - and Pinterest is a newcomer that's generating excitement.

Facebook

Facebook is one of the best known social networking sites. It began in 2004 as a way for college students to stay in touch and has grown to 1,200 employees and 400 million active users, with more every day.

Facebook's self-proclaimed mission is to give people the power to share and make the world more open and connected. People use it to tell others about their company, service or product, but at this time, it's still more a social, rather than business, oriented network. However, Facebook is striving to monetize and that means more business engagement.

Once you sign up and get an account with Facebook, you can search for people you know who have a Facebook profile and connect with them by asking them to be your "friend".

Once they accept, you each have access to the other's profile, where you can read postings about what they are up to, post comments on their wall and see comments from their other Facebook "friends".

You can also send semi-private messages and correspond with instant messaging, if they are online the same time you are.

After you make a few "friends" you begin to get suggestions from Facebook for additional "friends". These might be people you know or people who know people you know.

One of the big objections to Facebook newcomers is that the activity can be overwhelming. Especially if you're the type of person who wants to read every post.

It helps if you think of Facebook like a big cocktail party.

At this party, you have a presence, a profile, and you can interact with a variety of people. As you drift from group to group, you find some are discussing the weather, some politics, some business and others are looking to hook up.

With this concept in mind, the loose structure and often trivial conversations are more tolerable.

You wouldn't try to comment or even listen to every discussion, so you find the ones that interest you and interact with them.

If you've attended a cocktail party or Chamber mixer, you

know that what you get out of it is proportionate to what you put into it. You project professionalism, bring plenty of business cards and prepare a concise elevator speech.

In other words, you are prepared for opportunities.

However, just like a mixer, you'll be branded a boor if you use the opportunity to simply push your business.

The purpose of social networking is not to get business, it's to develop relationships.

If you were in real estate, you wouldn't introduce yourself at parties by asking strangers to buy a house from you, because it's rude.

Better to establish rapport, learn about them, share a bit about you, then they might ask about the house and be willing to hear you out.

Facebook also allows you to make business pages, previously called fan pages, which function differently than a profile.

There are also group pages and causes. Pages are suitable for public figures and businesses, while groups are good for smaller organizations and gatherings.

You have to have a personal profile before you can set up pages and you cannot have more than one personal profile.

Of course, this could all change tomorrow, because Facebook's most outstanding feature is that it never stays the same.

LinkedIn

LinkedIn is about business. Representing 150 industries and 200 countries, it connects experienced professionals with each other. LinkedIn says that over 60 million professionals use the network to exchange information, ideas and opportunities.

LinkedIn has groups within it where members can participate and discuss industry issues, make new contacts and establish expertise.

There are some great discussions and the opportunity to offer your expertise in a helpful way. Also you can recommend people and they can do the same for you.

LinkedIn has a tighter friend network, with emphasis on actually knowing people with whom you connect. This makes the connections more meaningful as they are harder to come by.

LinkedIn demographics are professional, business-minded, educated people.

Twitter

See What's Happening Right Now - that's Twitter's current tagline, and immediately tells you that Twitter is timely and fast-moving.

Twitter seems to be the hardest for those who are new to social media to get. It's the best known micro-blogging site, which is when you publish small pieces of digital information and share it with a group of people.

It's somewhat comparable to texting on your mobile phone. Texting is communicating by typing short messages, usually under 160 characters. It's immediate and addicting.

Twitter is like texting the messages on a grand scale.
When you set up your account, you choose people to follow, which means when they tweet, or post, you will see that information.

They might, or might not, follow you back. There is no obligation, such as in Facebook or LinkedIn, to be mutually connected.

Celebrities love Twitter for this very reason. They can have one way conversations with their fans, or two-way conversations if they decide to follow them back, which they usually don't.

Ashton Kutcher, for example, has over 10 million followers, but only follows 690.

Because of this broadcasting ability, Twitter is also become a news source in catastrophic situations such as earthquakes and floods. People at the scene report as things happen, tweeting and sending video clips that are instantly picked up, re-tweeted and spread through social networks like Facebook, YouTube and even traditional media outlets.

Tweets can bring world attention to an event and mobilize help. There's a website, called breakingtweets.com - *world news Twitter style* -where the latest news and comments from twitterers are available.

If Facebook is a cocktail party, Twitter has been compared to a water cooler. A very big water cooler. There are about 70 million people on Twitter, generating around a billion tweets per month.

Twitter is a good tool for promoting content and making connections. It works well for those who can benefit from being able to send short information to a large group of people.

Restaurants use Twitter to invite their customers to follow them, then keeping them updated on daily specials and events. It works because the customers already have an interest in the restaurant, and by giving them a convenient way to have updates, it's perceived as a service and benefit.

Businesses used to create focus groups to get feedback on new products or ideas before they spent thousands of dollars to develop them. You can create your own focus group if you have a strong Twitter following. Try tossing something out there and see what comes back. People like to share great ideas just for the fun of it.

Your Twitter account can feed into your Facebook and other social network pages, as well as your website, allowing you to update everything with one post.

The caution here is that while Twitter is a place to post frequently, you probably don't want to feed every tweet to LinkedIn or Facebook. On Twitter, tweeting constantly isn't offensive. That's a different approach than you use for Facebook or similar sites.

Plus, Facebook prefers you post directly.

However, if you want to update several locations at once, there are ways to connect your social media channels to automatically broadcast messages.

You can write all your tweets at once but have them go out at predetermined times during the day. Services like Gremlin allow you to schedule and broadcast later.

Tweetdeck is a desktop application you can download and read incoming tweets, post a tweet, set it up to automatically shorten long URL addresses (important because you only have 160 words), schedule posts and do other nifty things.

YouTube

Online video is becoming more popular as consumers turn to it for news, entertainment and information. It's estimated adults between 18-24 watch over five hours of video a month, and as content increases, the hours will continue to increase.

YouTube is owned by Google and is often used as a search engine.

You can subscribe to channels you like and get notification of new uploads.

The video quality is inconsistent. On one extreme, people can upload video they took on their cell phones, and on the other there are professional agencies uploading what they hope will become the next viral marketing hit.

Videos can be embedded in websites, blogs and social networks like Facebook. If popular, they'll spread by word of mouth as people share them with friends.

In addition to marketing, videos can also be training tools, allowing people to learn by watching and hearing the instructions.

Embedding video in your blog post can increase traffic to your site.

Pinterest

Pinterest is a newcomer but it's growing fast. The demographics show it appeals to primarily to woman, and it's very visual.

You join Pinterest by invitation, but once you are on it you can follow people and set up categories of thing you love.

There's lots of discussion about using Pinterest for business, but at this moment it's mostly social. You can sign in using Facebook or Twitter and all of the sudden your Facebook and Twitter connections will start to show up.

It could be a nice support network to amplify your existing connections.

OTHER MEDIA

Podcasting

The word podcasting came from combining iPod (Apple's MP3 player) and broadcasting. However, the MP3 or MP4 files are not limited to use on the iPod or iPad.

Almost any computer or digital media player can play the audio files.

Subscribers sign up for their favorite podcasts using an RSS feed, the same way they subscribe to blogs, and the episodes are delivered to them.

To make a podcast you simply use a recording program for your computer, save the file in the correct format and upload to your site.

Video podcasts merge audio and video, and can be subscribed to the same way as an audio podcast. Producing one takes a camera, editing software and access to the Internet.

Have you ever wanted to have your own call-in, live radio show?

Podcasts are the answer. Services like Blog Talk Radio put things together to make it easy.

Blog Talk Radio offers the capability for scheduled shows, audience participation, live and archived broadcasts and syndication.

Webinars/Teleconferencing

Online seminars, or teleconferences, are a great way to introduce your product or service, or train your clients in the use of the same.

Companies use these techniques to give potential clients a taste of their services for free so people can determine if the product or service is right for them.

A webinar, or online seminar, is a virtual meeting using your computer. It can be audio only, such as a teleconference, or audio and visual. It can be small, with a handful of attendees, or number in the thousands.

Typically a live webinar has opportunities for the audience to interact, either by posting their questions or comments or by asking audibly through their phone or Internet connection.

The host can mute the audience to cut down on background noise and unmute select participants when they indicate a question or comment.

The event is usually recorded and available for playback later.

Handouts can be sent out prior to the meeting or after it, with relevant links and additional follow-up information that enriches the experience.

There are free teleconferencing services and paid webinar providers from which to choose, depending upon your needs.

e-Newsletters

Electronic newsletters, or e-Newsletters, can leverage your other marketing by keeping your business name in front of the customer and bringing some type of benefit right to their in-box on a regular basis. When you show an interest in your customer and their needs, you begin to establish yourself as the one they will turn to first to solve their problem.

Building customer loyalty makes good sense, since studies show that it can cost as much as five times more to acquire a new customer than to maintain existing ones.

Repeat customers spend twice as much as new customers, so the wise businessperson cultivates that relationship.

One way to do that is to stay in touch on a regular basis.

An e-Newsletter is generally delivered on a per-determined schedule and can be weekly, monthly, semi-annually – whatever works best for your needs.

It's an opportunity to give updates, links, introduce new products/services, new staff, business changes that affect your readers or other news. You'll want to have interesting, useful information and refrain from bombarding your reader with relentless advertising pitches.

E-Newsletters have an advantage over hard-copy, snail-mail newsletters because they save you money on printing and postage.

According to Constant Contact, an e-mail marketing company, e-Newsletters have a response rate of five times greater than direct mail.

There's another benefit. When you send a paper newsletter through the mail, you don't know if anyone receives it, opens it or reads it.

With e-Newsletters, you can track all of that.

Here's how it works. You begin by building a list of subscribers. The e-Newsletter will be sent to their e-mail addresses, and that subjects the entire process to the CAN-SPAM act.

The CAN-SPAM is regulated by the Federal Trade Commission and sets the rules for commercial e-mail.

The rules include the right for recipients to say no to your mailings and enacts tough penalties of up to $16,000 per violation if you do not comply.

This covers all e-mail which has the primary purpose of advertising or promoting a product or service, including business-to-business e-mail and contacting previous customers.

The requirements are common sense.

Make sure you clearly identify yourself with the originating domain name and e-mail address, as well as a valid postal address (street or PO box is acceptable).

Use subject lines that accurately describe your message. Disclose that your message is an ad.

Give your recipient a clear way to opt out of any future e-mail, and make sure you act upon an opt out within 10 business days.

It's your responsibility to ensure these rules are followed, even if you have contracted with another company to handle your e-mail marketing.

To find out more, you can visit the ftc.gov website, but it's very difficult to locate the information. As an alternative, try searching the term "CAN SPAM act" on your favorite search engine.

The easiest way to make sure you don't have any problems with compliance is to use a service that specializes in e-mail marketing. The resource section at the end of the book offers some suggestions.

A reputable service will have built-in safeguards to make sure your business meets all the necessary requirements.

In addition to e-mail newsletters, an e-mail marketing company can provide event marketing, the ability to take surveys and run autoresponders.

Event marketing provides the tools for sending out invitations, taking registration and even limiting attendance if necessary.

Surveys can help you find out what your customers are looking for, how well you are meeting their needs and even evaluate a new product or service. People like interactive opportunities, and surveys are a chance to give you feedback.

Autoresponders are even more fun.

Once known only for the automated e-mail response that were set when someone was out of town or unavailable, autoresponders in e-mail marketing offer a great way to provide information and customer benefits.

An autoresponder campaign would work like this. After a customer purchases your product or service, you can set up an autoresponder to check in with them after a period of time to make sure everything is going well, then you might remind them at a designated period to replace something or service it.

Another application would be to offer a course or support material delivered every week for a number of weeks.

Autoresponders can be set up to send e-mails at designated times after a client has signed up.

For example, once someone signs up to purchase a software program, an autoresponder might follow up a few days later to make sure the person was able to download the program and see if there were any questions.

After that, an autoresponder might touch base a couple weeks later to offer instruction on a product feature the customer might not have tried yet.

All this could be set up once for every customer and would be triggered by the initial registration. It's a great way to stay in touch.

CLAIM YOUR BUSINESS ONLINE

Check your listing on Google, Google Places, Yahoo, etc. If you haven't done so, claim your business listing. You can simply follow the directions given on each site.

A few other online directories to check:
Bingbusinessportal.com (beta)
Biz.yelp.com
Bozemandirect.info
CityDirect.info
CitySearch.com
Dex Knows – call 1-877-433-9249
listings.local.yahoo.com - free basic listing
Manta.com
Superpages.com
YP.com - only good if you have a land line

LOCATION-BASED MARKETING

The popularity of location-based marketing is growing, driven by applications such as Foursquare, Gowalla, Facebook Places, oopt, Yelp, BrightKite and many others.

It's most popular among a younger demographic.

Location based marketing is spurred by providing users with incentives for checking in. You should identify your target market segments, then create appropriate rewards. You should think about tiered reward systems, and mechanisms that delight users by allowing them to uncover better offers and special rewards. Create a relevant offer for participants.

The older demographic is not indicating much interest, and I don't think that's going to change. However, I do believe we will be dragged into it as the options to participate online are no longer going to be available unless you activate your location.

For businesses, if you have a physical address, make sure you have it posted everywhere, as the idea is that people looking for pizza, for example, will search geographically and you'll want to be found.

NON-TECHNICAL PROMOTION

Volunteering

Volunteering is a wonderful way to share your expertise and show people that you are knowledgeable.

Not only that, but we like to do business with those we know, like and trust.

Nothing builds trust like actually working side-by-side with someone to accomplish a common goal. Even though you're not getting paid, you'll want to behave like you are, because how you handle yourself in situations like this tells others what you'll be like if they do business with you.

The word of mouth generated by your attitude, willingness and contribution is powerful and you want to make sure it's positive, too. Treat your volunteer assignments with the same professionalism and care as you would your biggest client.

Plus it just feels good.

Opportunities can be found through your local business or nonprofit organizations.

Writing a Book

Nearly every business owner can benefit from writing a book. If you plan on speaking to promote your company or service, a book will help you secure more engagements.

A book helps you establish credibility, it informs and educates your readers and it gives them the opportunity to get to know you.

Someone who enjoys your book will be more likely to do business with you, so books are an excellent way to attract new prospects.

Book sales provide an additional revenue stream to your business, one that does not require your active participation in order to bring in money.

Thanks to the Internet, people can purchase books anytime of day or night, and in the case of an e-book, download it instantly with no effort on your part.

The opportunities for publishing have grown tremendously over the past few years. While traditional publishing still carries some cachet, the pragmatic writer would be wise to check into some of the alternatives.

Depending upon your goal for the book, you may find satisfying and lucrative options for publication outside the traditional route.

However, contrary to the nonsense you find hyped online, writing a decent book is not easy. If you haven't got the time and skill, hire a ghostwriter.

Although a good ghostwriter costs money, a Skinny Budget Marketer weighs the ROI. If having a book published under your name would be a significant business boost, it's a worthwhile expense.

Public Speaking

Speaking is another way to promote your business or service. Many organizations are looking for speakers.

While budgets are tight, they may not have much, if any, for an honorarium, but the opportunity to connect with a large group of people at once could offset the lack of remuneration.

If you have books or product you could sell, check with the organization to see if you can bring them. If nothing else, make sure you have handouts, brochures or business cards available to make it easy for interested listeners to contact you later.

If speaking scares you, or you don't have good public speaking skills, Toastmasters International is an organization that provides training and weekly practice for a low membership cost.

News Releases

News releases broadcast information about your company that is topical, timely and interesting. If you have a new product line, a news release will inform the media and possibly reap rewards in the form of articles, interviews and publicity.

Often referred to as "press releases" because you had to use the press as your distribution outlet, the term has evolved into "news releases'" to underscore the fact that you can now distribute the information yourself. The same rules that applied when preparing press releases still applies today.

You must have a newsworthy message. While it's great to generate as many releases as you can, each one must offer interesting, topical, valuable information in order to get noticed.

Write with Search Engine Optimization (SEO) in mind, but remember your news must appeal to the human readers in order to generate action and don't overdo it.

SEO friendly tips include:

- Keep your title between 2-22 words.

- Keep your message on target and brief. Aim for between 350 to 550 words. Make sure you include the relevant details and stay focused on your purpose. One clear message per news release.

- Take advantage of links. One major way Internet news releases differ from the traditional printed release is in the ability to link the key words. Don't overdo it. One or two links is about right. Too many and you will defeat yourself.
Use clear, factual language. Avoid jargon or inside terminology.

- Provide complete contact information. The name of the person to contact, phone number, e-mail address, physical address, website, fax number.

The goal is to make it easy for reporters to work with you. The average reader will spend less than 10 seconds scanning your release, so it's important to make it effective.

PROVEN CLASSICS AND SMART TIPS

There are some marketing techniques that have stood the test of time and should have a place in your strategy.

Professional organizations are still a great way to make personal contacts and business connections. Meeting face-to-face with others who share your interests, socializing and having a common goal is a powerful way to build alliances and relationships.

There are local organizations and online organizations. Often people join online organizations, make friends and get a chance to meet at annual conventions or conferences. You can find a list by using your favorite search engine.

Sampling, or offering consumers a chance to try your product or service, is another tried-and-true technique that pays dividends. This technique works because it addresses a major concern. One reason people hesitate when considering a purchase is the fear of the unknown.

Why not remove the risk for your target market by offering a sample of what they can expect? With a little creativity, you'll discover this is possible with almost any product or service. Remember in the beginning when you defined what your business was and what you were really selling? That can help you figure out what a meaningful sample might look like.

A real estate agent can't give a sample of a house, but what is the agent's real business? Selling themselves. And when they offer to provide a free market analysis, for example, they are giving a sample of their service. A buyer or seller can evaluate the agent's presentation, professionalism and reputation to make a wise choice.

Referrals can grow your business and all you have to do is ask. When you make a client happy, solve their problem or help them in some way, ask them if there is any one else they know who might benefit from the same service? If they love your product, ask them who else might want a product like that?

Earlier we talked about how people enjoy telling their friends about good deals, great products or exceptional service.

But sometimes they get busy or don't think about it. Asking is just a gentle nudge. Don't push, be gracious and thankful if they are willing to suggest a few friends.

When you have a happy client, remember to ask for a testimonial. These can be displayed on your website and used in your promotional materials.

Cooperative or complementary marketing is a way to partner with another company for mutual benefit. Find a business that serves your clientele and propose a joint venture.

A bridal photographer might work with an event planner to host a seminar about planning the perfect wedding. Or a grocery store and local chef could team up to offer cooking classes.

Affiliate marketing is an online way to join forces with other businesses by linking to their websites, products and services from your own. In affiliate marketing, you would get a percentage of sales that result from your referrals.

Worth a look? Paid advertising on the Internet

Google has the DoubleClick Ad Planner, a free media planning tool to:

> Identify websites your target customer visit
> Define audiences by demographics and interests
> Search for websites relevant to your target audience
> Access unique users, page views, and other data
> Easily build media plans for yourself or your clients

Create lists of websites where you'd like to advertise
Get website statistics for your media plan

DoubleClick for Publishers (DFP) Small Business is a hosted ad serving solution that offers a toolkit to sell ads on your site through partners like AdSense and ad networks.

Google can offer this because, like Facebook, it has spent years collecting information about us and now it's going to use it to make money.

Which leads me to:

THE COST OF FREE - A CAUTIONARY TALE

Everyone loves getting something for nothing. The reality is that rarely does something come with no strings attached.

A few years ago (when credit was easy), I remember sitting in a salon next to a young woman getting her hair done for her wedding. She was chatty and excited as she told us all how she got a check in the mail from a national bank.

"Fifteen hundred dollars - made out to me!" she squealed. And went on to say how they were going to use it for their honeymoon.

This was one of those "teaser" loans offered in the form of a check and by cashing it, she unwittingly agreed to a punitive interest rate and a fat debt for her and her new husband after the honeymoon was over.

When enticed by the free , we have to look at what happens when the honeymoon is over.

In November of 2010 I read a quote on LifeHacker that has stuck with me:

"If you're not paying for the product, you ARE the product."

I thought of Facebook.

Facebook is not in the business of building your business, they are interested in monetizing theirs. Thanks to our giddy willingness to provide them with details about our lives we wouldn't even share with the Census takers, they have built a tremendous, accurate database with little expense to them.

Recently PC Magazine said it up this way: *"Facebook is an advertising company masquerading as a social network."*

Facebook has accumulating valuable information about all of us and now they are going to make big money from it.

The point? If you're going to play the game, you need to have eyes wide open. Understand that the tools you use to market your business, in many cases, are also using you to build theirs. Don't forget that.

As long as you know what's going on, and you choose it, then it's fair. I just believe you should understand the true cost of *free*.

I use free or low-cost tools all the time. Sometimes they

are free because the company is using my information, like Facebook, and other times it's a way of letting me sample their product or service. I like being able to try the product, use a limited version, take a seminar or read a book section for nothing before I buy it.

For small to mid-sized businesses one of the biggest frustrations with Facebook is that they change the game continuously. It's worse than the weather - wait five minutes and Facebook's morphed again.

This is hard because now it takes time to figure out the new rules, redesign the page and make other adjustments to stay current.

It seems they subscribe to the unusual theory that *increasing* friction builds loyalty. Either that or they believe they've become so important in our lives that we'll hang on no matter how fast the merry-go-round spins.

Remember that it's their product. Like the example earlier about free websites, you are investing time and money building your connects and providing information on someone else's business platform. They own it. They have the right to change and complicate it.

You have the right to decide if you want to participate.

Just because something's free doesn't make it bad - as long as you understand why it's free. The other thing you need to understand is the alliances.

When the TV show, Survivor, first appeared, it was fascinating to watch the alliances form and shift depending on where the biggest advantages were. In real life, alliances occur more often than we realize.

If you went to your local supermarket and saw a big display of local-brand bread with signs indicating how healthy and nutrient-packed the bread was, you might buy a loaf or two. You might tell your friends about how you discovered this great bread.

What you might not know is that the bread company had a large infusion of cash provided by the grocery chain. They are invested in each other's success. Does this cause you to question the truth of the claims about the bread? It does me.

When I rely on someone for the truth, I don't like to find out they are making money by steering me toward a certain conclusion.

Doctors who owned testing clinics came under sharp scrutiny when they would recommend certain tests over and over, and always send the patients to their own profitable testing facility. This was considered misleading.

Google Ventures has invested money in several marketing companies, such as HubSpot, SalesForce and others. Google Ventures has been investing in third-party SEO and SEM companies since 2007.

Does this affect the advice we're given from these "leaders" in the industry? Is it misleading?

Check into it and determine for yourself how much you feel you are being impacted by social media social engineering.

Don't forget that you are still in charge. When you choose your media channels, consider the learning and re-learning curve, and aggravation factor, when you measure the return on your investment.

PUTTING IT ALL TOGETHER

Remember the fish business example we talked about in the Positioning section?

For your hypothetical fish business, your USP is that you sell peace of mind in a chaotic world.

One of your primary markets is the health industry, because research has shown that there are measurable benefits to having fish in a waiting room, that medical professionals appreciate the value and they can afford to hire you to install and maintain the aquarium.

Brainstorm some ways you can reach them (note: when you brainstorm you let the ideas flow and don't censor the bad ones, that comes later). Here's what you come up with:

> cold calls (ugh)
> newspaper ad
> radio
> TV
> Facebook
> Twitter

LinkedIn
demonstrations
speaking
professional organizations
white paper
training
blog/website
videos

These possibilities come from the research you've done, what you think is customary and the media with which you are most comfortable.

It's not a perfect list, but it's a starting point. Even though you can't stand cold calls, you included them because a sales course you once took said you had to do cold calls to get business.

You're not sure about the effectiveness of newspapers, radio or TV, but they're traditional. Since you love learning and sharing information, you included related activities.

Now look at your target customer? Who are they and where could you reach them?

Start with what you know. You already have two doctors as customers. They like you, and are willing to share ideas over a cup of coffee.

You find out both of them have a LinkedIn profile but see Facebook and Twitter as unimportant. They belong to a local leadership group.

They like facts backed up with research. They're active in the community. They don't watch TV, but they listen to satellite radio. They avoid salespeople but have formed close relationships with members of volunteer groups. They want to improve the patient experience.

It's likely their peers are similar.

Review your list and delete the things that don't apply for this campaign.

Then consider what you can do to forge connections.

You can gather research about the value of fish in medical settings – a white paper. Feature it on your website as a bonus, e-mail them a link.

Get involved with local volunteer groups, even in a support capacity. Perhaps you could provide something aquatic for an event, such as pool toys for the local therapy group.

Find out if the leadership group they belong to is looking for speakers and give an awesome presentation.

Offer a workshop on fish maintenance. Add content to your website directed specifically on aquariums in professional settings. Give tips and suggestions in a podcast. Record video demonstrations.

Write down these tasks, along with the estimated time you'll need. Break it down into bite-sized nuggets.

For example: To write a white paper you have to do research, which will take an hour, then write it, another hour. To make a video spin-off, another hour.

Take out your work schedule and start plugging the time into available slots. This might be a reality check as you realize you only have three hours a week, and your plan will take 20 hours.

Can you delegate some of it? The research? The writing?

You might have to revise your plan, eliminate some items, in order to accomplish what you want within your time frame. Or you might want to reset your deadline.

When you've finished allocating the tasks, you have a plan in place and know you'll get it done because you know when you'll be doing the steps to achieve it.

You can feel confident you'll accomplish your goal without feeling overwhelmed.

Duplicate this process for each promotion you create.

You're on your way.

Perfecting

This section on Perfecting is about taking care of what you have and growing it. Despite the name, I don't believe it will ever be *perfect,* however my dictionary explains "perfecting" is to refine and polish.

That works for me.

What can you do to manage your systems, evaluate your progress and strengthen your business?

CULTIVATE THE CUSTOMER

Don't ignore the obvious. Your existing customers are valuable assets and it makes sense to nurture that relationship.

Have a follow-up system, both for leads and for existing customers. Stay in touch through regular e-mails and phone calls. Offer them something special to let them know you appreciate them.

Keep them in mind as you go through your business day. If you are attending an event and think it could benefit one of your clients, invite them. If you read an interesting article you think they'll find useful, send it to them.

Connect them. If you introduce them and they can help each

other, you're the hero. That kind of consideration goes a lot farther than lip service to show you truly care about their success, especially when there's no direct benefit for you.

When feasible, include your best clients in your business development. Give them a chance to give input on a new product or service. Get their ideas about how you can improve an offering.

People like to feel valued and they like to offer their opinions. If they're good clients, they probably have some terrific ideas and all you have to do is talk to them.

I can guarantee that if you develop a product or service from client input, they'll be your biggest fans and tell everyone they know. They're now invested in your success, the same way you are in theirs.

TEST, MONITOR AND TRACK YOUR RESULTS

Don't be afraid to experiment!

Testing different strategies and tactics encourages growth and makes you the expert on your company. You gain a better understanding of your customers, their behavior, preferences, and how everything works together to create a profitable strategy.

Run two different promotions to see which brings more business. Try split e-mail campaigns, different offers and advertising.

Evaluate what works and what doesn't and adjust your marketing accordingly.

Use the Internet to notify you when your name comes up. Set up Google alerts for your business name and you'll get e-mail updates of the latest relevant Google results from sources such as news, web, blogs, video and groups. Use Social Mention, which is like Google alerts but for social media, with real time social media search and analysis.

Plug blog articles into Digg and StumbleUpon. Follow users that follow you.

Skinny Budget Marketers constantly test and analyze in order to know what is working and what isn't.

Don't try to measure everything. Pick 2-4 social media metrics to try. If you add a new one, drop an old one.

Don't get lost in the process of data acquisition. It's called "analysis paralysis", when you get frozen by statistics. There's a limit to the amount of data that you can absorb and apply.

Sometimes too much tracking is worse than too little. Choose a measurement system you're comfortable with that helps you increase your effectiveness, improve your service and multiply your profits.

The arguments for how much time you should devote to measurement is debatable.

The fact is, the weight you give to metrics and the amount of time you spend on analytics could be more related to whether you are right-brained or left-brained than anything else.

You'll want to use some system to evaluate the effectiveness of your advertising, marketing, social media and promotions.

It's a tool, to help you make better decisions so you can fulfil your real goal: Growing your business.

Use what you learn to refine your efforts, define your customer and perfect your application.

MISCELLANEOUS

Be Found

Put your contact information on everything.

I know. I said this before, but it amazes me how people forget this basic wisdom.

If you've ever received an invoice and you've had questions, only to discover there is no phone number or e-mail address present, you appreciate the importance of contact information. By the time you track down how to reach the company, in order to get an answer so you can PAY them, you're peeved.

Keep a Notebook

Nearly every one of the digital marketing channels you use requires a user name and password. I can't tell you how many times I've had to help a client set up new login credentials because they couldn't find that vital information.

Do yourself a huge favor and immediately set up a marketing notebook where you can keep track of everything.

I've tried several different systems over the years, and settled on a small, loose-leaf binder with alphabetical tabs. One page per, with the name at the top, the user name and password, and any instructions that I'll need later.

Trust me, if you don't access the information often, you'll forget the procedure, or where to go once you log on, or how you made the changes the last time. Make these notes here, so everything's in one place.

I also designate pages for media I find interesting but aren't ready to try, with notes on why I think it would be a useful tool for the future.

This way when I come across a great program or potential market I won't lose the idea. I know where I put it and can find it if and when I do have the need for it.

With my notes, I'll also be reminded why it appealed to me.

BUSINESS HEALTH

Every so often run a diagnostic on the state of your business and give it a tune-up if necessary.

The SWOT Analysis can give you a realistic picture of where

you are and what you need to do to reinforce the strengths and minimize the threats.

While you're at it, take a look at your receivables and payables and eliminate the deadwood. While these aren't marketing tools, your skinny budget will get a boost and your business will grow with attention to these details.

CONGRATULATIONS!

YOU'VE EARNED YOUR 5-P DEGREE

Preparing
Positioning
Presenting
Promoting
Perfecting

You've complete the Skinny Budget Marketers 5P's of success.

You understand the concepts and benefits of using social media, Internet marketing and traditional media and how they work together to achieve synergy.

You've created a strategic marketing plan and picked tactics to reach your objectives.

You have a mantra and concise definition of your business and purpose.

You developed a customer archetype, or several, so you can gear your marketing to a real human being.

You've expanded your vocabulary to include business and marketing terms.

You now understand the importance of content, how to write it and where to get ideas.

And finally, you have a marketing plan that's manageable and a direction that makes sense.

You are a Skinny Budget Marketer, bound for success and ready to excel!

Thank you for buying my book.

I'd love to hear from you. Let me know how these techniques and methods are working in your business.

I am writing and publishing constantly, and am developing a line of business books you might like. These often come from my client's questions or challenges, so please share your ideas.

To get the current status of my progress and info on what's available, please join the Skinny Budget Marketing Club - on my website*.

You can connect with me on LinkedIn, Twitter, Facebook and Pinterest - go to my website* for the details and links. If you're new to social media, let me know when you connect and I'll be mindful.

If you like the book and find it helpful, please tell your friends!

Consider writing a review on Amazon (instructions on my site*). Thanks again for your support.

PLEASE visit my website for all the above and more:

*WorksbyDesign.com

Warmest Regards, Lynn

www.ingramcontent.com/pod-product-compliance
Lightning Source LLC
Chambersburg PA
CBHW060615210326
41520CB00010B/1349